Bo Goes Fishing

Story by Maribeth Boelts

Illustrations by Nikki Boetger

One morning, Bo saw a poster at the fishing store.

"There's a fishing contest tomorrow!" said Bo. "Whoever catches the biggest fish wins two new fishing poles and a trophy!"

"Let's try!" said Zak. "Do you have fishing poles?"

"No," said Bo.

"Hooks, bobbers, and worms?" asked Zak.

"No," said Bo. "We can make the poles, and I know how to get everything else."

Bo found the owner of the fishing store.

"If we sweep your sidewalks, would you let us use some of your hooks and bobbers for the fishing contest?" Bo asked.

"It's a deal!" said the owner.

At home, Bo looked for strong branches to use for the fishing poles.

Zak found clear string in his art supplies.

They got their fishing poles ready.

"That's it!" said Zak.
"Now we need to find worms."

"I'll find some," said Bo. He dug in the garden and pulled a fat worm from the ground.

The next morning, Bo and Zak went to the lake. Bo brought snacks, and Zak brought his camera.

They rowed to the middle of the lake and began to fish.

Bo's bobber bounced and swirled
around in the water.

"I have a bite!" Bo said,
pulling in a little fish.

Then Zak's bobber took a dip and dive,
and he pulled in another little fish.

Hours passed,
and the sun grew hot.
Soon Bo and Zak were
alone on the lake.

Bo caught one more fish,
even smaller than the others.

"One, two, three fish," Bo counted.

"One blue, one green, and one orange fish," said Zak.

"And all of them are too little to win the contest!" said Bo.

Just then, Bo and Zak heard a giant SPLASH!
They turned and saw the tail of a huge fish.

"Look at that tail!" said Zak.
"That is one big fish!"

"Let's row!" said Bo.
"We can catch him!"

They rowed and raced to the spot of the splash. But the fish was gone.

Then they saw a SPLASH across the lake.

"That big fish is fast!" said Zak.

They rowed and raced again.

"He keeps swimming away!"
said Bo.

"I'm tired of chasing him," said Zak.

"Me, too," said Bo. "We can fish here, but there's only one worm left."

"You can fish," said Zak. "I'll eat a snack."

Bo threw out his line, but his bobber snagged a log. When he pulled, the fishing line snapped.

"We're out of worms," said Bo.

"We're out of luck, too," said Zak.

Suddenly, Bo and Zak saw a **SPLASH!**

"The big fish is back!" exclaimed Bo.

Then the big fish jumped again, right next to the boat.

"He's getting closer!" exclaimed Zak.

The big fish jumped once more.
This time, he flew high above the boat,
flicked his huge tail, and . . .

With a plop and a flop, he landed in the boat!

"This must be the biggest fish in the lake!"
exclaimed Bo. "Quick! Take a picture!"

Zak took a picture of Bo with the big fish.

"This fish could win the prize!" Zak said.

The big fish flipped and flopped.
Bo almost dropped him.

"He's trying to jump back into the lake,"
said Zak.

Bo was quiet. "That's where he belongs," he said. "Let's set him free so he can go home."

"And the little fish, too," Zak said.

The two friends helped the big fish and the three little fish slip into the water.

With a slap of their tails, they were gone.

At the fishing store, Bo and Zak
told everyone about the big fish.

"Did that really happen?"
asked the owner.

"I took a picture of it,"
said Zak. "Take a look!"

Everyone crowded
around Zak's camera.

"Bo and Zak did not *keep* the biggest fish of the day, but they did *catch* it!" said the owner.

"And for that, they win the contest!"
he said.

Glossary

find

jump

pull

look

big

little

blue

one

green

two

orange

three

The Learnalots™

Bo
Literacy

Kit
Math

Piper
Music and Movement

Sofie
Social and Emotional Skill

Flora
Nature

Scout
Health and Fitness

Leo
Science

Zak
Art and Creativity

BrightStart Learning
7342 11th Ave. NW
Seattle, WA 98117
www.brightstartlearning.com

Developed in conjunction with Trillium Publishing, Inc.

Illustrations created by Nikki Boetge

ISBN: 978-1-938751-01-1

Printed and bound in China.

10 9 8 7 6 5 4 3 2 1